CONCISE OBJECT SERMONS
FOR CHILDREN

CONCISE OBJECT SERMONS FOR CHILDREN

ROBERT S. COOMBS

BAKER BOOK HOUSE
Grand Rapids, Michigan 49516

ISBN: 0-8010-2541-9

Second printing, February 1991

Printed in the United States of America

Scripture references in this volume are from the Revised Standard
Version, © Copyright 1946, 1952, 1971, 1973 by Thomas Nelson, Inc., New
York. Used by permission.
"In Living Color" (chapter 41) by Camille Watts is used by permission.
"A Brighter Light" (chapter 42) by Kevin Cramer is used by permission.
"My True Friends" (chapter 43) by Chrissy Calloway and Barsha Elkins is
used by permission.

To

Amy Marie and **Andrew Stephen**

Who have brought the words of Jesus to life

"Of such is the kingdom of God"

Contents

Introduction

Including a children's sermon as part of the worship service will add an extremely worthwhile and meaningful dimension to worship. Not only will the children feel that they have an important and vital place in the service, but the adults will also gain new insights to simple and yet profound truths.

As stated in my first book, *Of Such Is the Kingdom: Object Sermons for Children* (with Iris Perry), a few guidelines are noteworthy regarding the development and delivery of a good children's sermon. Please consider these suggestions:

1. If possible, have a designated area where you may sit and allow the children to gather around you. This provides the opportunity for closeness, eye-to-eye contact, and comfortable dialogue.

2. Begin each children's sermon in the same manner. This will allow each child to know what to expect and thus should prove relaxing. For example, I begin with a cheerful "good morning!" The children have become accustomed to this and respond with a hearty "good morning" of their own.

3. A good children's sermon, like all good sermons, has one point and one point only. Many children's sermons suffer greatly because the minister seeks to make more than one point.

4. The children are the intended audience of the ser-

mon. Therefore keep your one point simple and easy to understand for the group you are addressing. (The adults will still benefit greatly from the simple truth expressed!)

5. Make your point in two to three minutes. Since a child's attention span is relatively short, even the very best sermon can be ruined by the failure to keep it brief.

6. Encourage interaction. The richest joy of this special time of worship will be the response of the children in your group. The opportunity to participate speaks directly to a child's worth. The feelings of self-worth and importance given to a child in this setting may well carry into adulthood.

7. Enjoy yourself. Preparation and delivery of good children's sermons will bring such a worthwhile variety of results, they could well become a book in their own right.

"Whoever receives one such child
in my name receives me;
and whoever receives me,
receives not me but him who sent me."
Mark 9:37

1

Helping the Hurts

Text: "God is our refuge and strength, a very present help in trouble" (Ps. 46:1).

Object: Box of Band-Aids or other adhesive strips

Theme: God helps us when we hurt on the inside.

Today I have something with me that I know each one of you has needed at one time or another. Can you tell me what is inside this little can? [*Allow the children to respond.*] You are right! Inside are Band-Aids (or adhesive strips) of all shapes and sizes. Maybe a few of you could tell us about a time when you needed one. [*Allow a few children to share a story.*] It's sad to hear how some of you have been hurt at one time or another, but it's great to know there are bandages to cover your hurt places when you cut or scratch yourself.

If you were to fall down next week and let's say you scraped your knee or cut your finger, all you would have to do is ask your mommy or daddy to open a bandage like this and put it on your hurt place. [*Demonstrate by wrapping an adhesive strip around a child's finger while you talk.*] Of course, adding a special kiss is always a great help. With a kiss and a bandage, before you know it your hurt place will feel much, much better.

As nice as bandages are for hurt places like a scrape on the knee or a cut on the finger, they are really not much help for some other kinds of hurt. For example, suppose a friend says some really unkind words to you such as "I don't like you anymore," or "You are dumb," or "I think you are ugly." That can really hurt, but it's different from the hurt we feel when we cut or scratch ourselves. The hurt we feel comes from the sadness inside us. There are other times when we feel sad. Can you remember feeling sad when a friend you loved very much moved away, or your pet was hit by a car? That can really hurt by making us feel especially sad on the inside.

When we hurt on the inside, God can really help. Like a bandage that Mommy or Daddy gives you to feel better, God gives you his love to help *you* feel better. One of the best things about God is that no matter how much we hurt on the inside, his love can make us feel much, much better.

This morning I have a bandage for each of you to take home. When you use yours to help a hurt you feel on the outside, remember how God helps you when you feel a hurt on the inside. Let's thank God for loving us and helping us to feel better when we hurt on the inside.

Dear God, thank you for giving us bandages that help us feel better when we hurt on the outside. But thank you most of all for loving us and helping us to feel better when we hurt on the inside. Amen.

2

A Fish Out of Water

Text: "Jesus said to him, 'I am the way, and the truth, and the life; no one comes to the Father, but by me'" (John 14:6).

Object: Fish in a bowl

Theme: As much as a fish needs water, each of us needs Jesus.

Good morning. [*Allow the children to respond.*] This morning I have a little friend with me. Can anyone tell me what kind of friend this is? [*Allow the children to respond.*] Of course, my little friend is a fish. My fish's name is Flipper. Flipper is a great friend to have. I love to watch him swim around and around. Don't you think Flipper is just about the prettiest little fish you have ever seen?

I wonder, boys and girls, do you think Flipper ever gets tired of swimming around and around in this tiny little bowl? [*The children will probably agree that Flipper would be happier if he had more room.*] I know what we can do! Let's take Flipper out of this bowl. We can just put him right here on the carpet, and then we can have a great time playing together. Flipper will have all the room he needs. Wouldn't that be great? [*The children should be responding at this point.*] No? Why? Oh, I see. Flipper needs the water to live. If we took him out of the water, what would happen? [*Allow the children to explain.*] You are right. Flipper really needs this water, doesn't he? Without the water, Flipper could not live.

Boys and girls, thinking about how much Flipper needs this water reminds me of how much each of us needs Jesus. Just as much as Flipper needs water, we need Jesus. Without Jesus in our hearts, our lives would be as sad and as hopeless as a fish out of water.

Next time you see a little fish like Flipper happily swimming around in a bowl of water, think about how much that little fish needs water. Then remember, that just as much as a fish needs water, you need Jesus in your heart.

Dear God, help us to always remember that just as much as a fish needs water, we need your Son, Jesus. Amen.

3
Good and Clean

Text: "From the same mouth come blessing and cursing. My brethren, this ought not to be so" (James 3:10).

Object: Toothbrush

Theme: Say only clean words of kindness and never dirty words of ugliness.

How many of you brushed your teeth before coming to church this morning? Everybody remembered to brush their teeth. That's great! Tell me something. Why do you need to brush your teeth? [*Allow the children to respond.*] Oh, I see. Brushing your teeth does help keep them clean. What do you suppose would happen if you stopped brushing your teeth? [*Allow adequate time for the children to expound on the hazards of not brushing their teeth.*] Exactly, your teeth would get very, very dirty. Before long, you might even get little holes in your teeth called "cavities." After getting the cavities in your teeth, if you wait long enough before brushing again, your teeth will become dirtier and dirtier and then start to decay and finally, when they are really rotten, they will fall right out of your mouth. Knowing what can happen if you do not brush your teeth, do you think it is important to brush your teeth? [*The children should give a hearty response.*] Right. It is very, very important to keep your teeth nice and clean. Every day, after you eat and before bedtime, you should take a toothbrush like this and brush your teeth until they are sparkling clean.

Let me ask you something. Suppose you brush your teeth after every meal and keep them sparkling clean, do you think that would help keep the words that come out of your mouth nice and clean too? [*The children will respond with the obvious answer.*] Of course not. No matter how clean we keep our teeth, we can still say some pretty dirty words. The kind of words I am talking about sound ugly and make others feel bad. The worst thing about saying dirty words is that if we say them long enough, *we* will become dirty and filthy inside. That is why Jesus taught us to say only clean words of kindness and never nasty words of ugliness.

I hope you will remember to keep your teeth sparkling clean. Each time you brush your teeth, think about keeping your words sparkling clean also.

Dear God, help us to only say clean words of kindness. Amen.

4

The Amazing Computer

Text: "What is man that thou art mindful of him, and the son of man that thou dost care for him? Yet thou hast made him little less than God, and dost crown him with glory and honor" (Ps. 8:4, 5).

Object: A computer and child's software program

Theme: God has given us minds to play, work, and learn.

Today I have an object with me that is one of the most exciting and amazing developments of our time. Can anyone tell me what this is? [*Allow the children to respond.*] Of course, this is a computer. What does a computer do? [*Most children will be aware of a variety of uses for computers. Allow them to share.*] Computers are really important because there is so much they can do. They are a lot of fun for playing games like Pac Man and Asteroids. They also help us with our work like writing letters or adding and subtracting numbers. One of the nicest accomplishments a computer does for children is helping them to learn new things.

This morning, I have a program in our computer that helps you learn how to read. Let's take a look. [*This is a Random House* "Snoopy's Reading Machine" *program for beginning readers. There are several children's learning programs on the market. Interact with the children as you play the particular software program you have chosen.*] This is a fun way to learn how to read. This computer knows when you have the wrong answer and also when you have the

18

right answer. Isn't it amazing how smart this computer is?

Boys and girls, let me share with you something that is even more amazing than this computer. God has given each of you a brain that is smarter than the smartest computer. The brain God has given you is even more important than a computer because it allows you to play and work and learn. With the brain God has given you, you can think like no computer can and you can do things no computer can. Let's thank God for giving to each of us our amazing brains.

Dear God, thank you for computers that help us to play and work and learn. Thank you even more for giving us minds that allow us to play and work and learn. Amen.

5
A Better Look

Text: " 'These things I have spoken to you, that my joy may be in you, and that your joy may be full' " (John 15:11).

Object: Kaleidoscope

Theme: Jesus gives special beauty to each of our lives.

The object I have with me this morning is one I believe some of you may have seen at one time or another. You can see that it has a long slender tube section and two wheels at the end, filled with different kinds of colored glass. Can anyone tell me what this is called? [*Allow the children a few guesses. If no one provides the correct answer, tell the children the name of the object and continue.*] Right. This is called a kaleidoscope. That's an awfully big word isn't it? Let's all try to say *kaleidoscope* together.

Now that you can say the word *kaleidoscope*, tell me, what does a kaleidoscope do? [*Allow the children to respond.*] Exactly. A kaleidoscope makes thousands of shapes in beautiful colors. All you have to do to make it work is look through this tube and turn the wheels. The light shining through the colored glass in the wheels makes the beautiful shapes and colors. [*Allow a few children to look. Tell the children that after they have left the sanctuary, every child will have the opportunity to view.*]

I love looking through my kaleidoscope because there seems to be an endless beauty of shapes and colors. Whenever I look through my kaleidoscope, I am reminded of why I love being a Christian. I love being a Christian because there seems to be endless beauty to my life. That is because when Jesus comes into our hearts and makes us Christians, we see the world in a new and beautiful way. In fact, like the kaleidoscope there is no end to the beauty that Jesus gives to every day of our lives.

Next time you are looking through a kaleidoscope think about Jesus and remember the special beauty he gives each of our lives.

Dear God, thank you for giving us Jesus who gives special beauty to each of our lives. Amen.

6

The Door to Life

Text: "'Behold, I stand at the door and knock; if any one hears my voice and opens the door, I will come in to him and eat with him, and he with me'" (Rev. 3:20).

Object: A door with a cross inscribed, or a large drawing of same.

Theme: Jesus is our way to God.

This morning I have a rather large object with me. Yes, it's a door, of course. Where are some of the places we find doors? [*Allow the children to respond.*] Everywhere we go we see doors. Regardless of where they are—in church, at home, in school, or the store—all doors are made for the same purpose. Why do we have doors? [*Allow the children to respond.*]

Because doors are so important for coming and going out of buildings and because doors are everywhere we look, a long, long time ago (about seven hundred years ago—that's before anyone of us here was born), a group of persons had a great idea. They decided to put a special design in their doors. Just about everyone liked their idea. In fact, it was such a great idea, many of the doors made today still have the same design. Look carefully at this door and see if you can guess what design is in this door. [*The children will probably not guess correctly. After a few guesses, continue with the message.*] There is a cross in this door. Let me show you where it is. Can you all see it now?

The persons who thought of putting a cross in the door

did so for a very important reason. Whenever we go through a door, they want us to see the cross and then to think about Jesus. That is a great idea, isn't it? Because in many ways Jesus is like a door. Like going through a door to find our way to a new place, through Jesus we find our way to God.

Next time you walk through a door, look for the cross. If you see one, think about Jesus, and as you make your way through that door, remember Jesus is our way to God.

Dear God, thank you for doors that remind us of Jesus, our special way to you. Amen.

7
It's About Time

Text: "Remember, O LORD, what the measure of life is, for what vanity thou hast created all men!" (Ps. 89:47).

Object: Hourglass

Theme: Using the time God gives us for the very best.

I have something with me that helps tell time. Can any of you tell me what this is? [*Allow the children to respond.*] You are such a smart group. You are right. This is an hourglass. How does an hourglass work? [*Allow the children to respond.*] Right. The sand slowly passes through this narrow passage in the glass. The sand has been falling since the beginning of our worship service. You can see how much has fallen through. Can anybody guess how long it will take all the sand to fall to the bottom? [*Allow the children to guess.*] You have made some great guesses. (Name) was the closest. It takes exactly one hour for all the sand to fall to the bottom. That's about the length of our worship service.

Watching this sand fall through this hourglass reminds us that each hour of every day we have only so much time. Time is one of the most precious gifts given by God. Because we have only so much time in every day, it is very, very important to use our time for the very best. What are some good ways to use our time? [*Several suggestions should be given, such as using time to work, play, and*

24

learn.] Make sure you use the time God gives you for the very best. Take time to play, work, and learn each and every day.

Dear God, help us to use the time you give us for the very best. Amen.

8

Keeping in Tune

Text: "Behold, how good and pleasant it is when brothers dwell in unity!" (Ps. 133:1).

Object: A children's choir

Theme: Everything works better when everyone works together.

What a happy day this is for us! Today we have our children's choir singing a song especially for us. Let's listen. [*The children's choir should sing the first verse of a familiar children's song such as* "Jesus Loves Me."] That was just beautiful. "Jesus Loves Me" is one of my favorite songs.

Boys and girls, wouldn't you like to hear our choir sing another verse of "Jesus Loves Me?" [*The children's choir should sing the second verse, but this time with one child purposefully singing loudly out of tune.*] Does that sound beautiful to you? [*The children will be quick to point out that the song has lost its beautiful sound.*] I wonder what is wrong? [*At least one child should suggest the problem— someone is singing out of tune.*] Isn't that amazing? Just one person singing out of tune has ruined our beautiful song. Let's hear our choir one more time. This time everyone will sing in tune together. [*The children's choir should sing the third verse in tune.*] That was beautiful, wasn't it?

I have learned an important lesson today, boys and girls. I have learned the importance of everyone in our choir singing in tune together. If one person chooses not to sing in tune with the others, the whole song is ruined. But when everyone works together, the sound that is produced is beautiful.

That's true, not just with choirs, but with everything. We should always try our best to work in tune with others. The more we stay in tune by trying to get along, the more beautiful everything will be. Let's ask God to help us always do our best to get along with others so we can stay in tune and work together for the very best.

Dear God, thank you for choirs that sing beautifully together and remind us of the importance of working together to produce the very best. Amen.

9
Don't Forget

Text: "Seek the LORD while he may be found, call upon him while he is near;" (Isa. 55:6).

Object: Pocket tape recorder

Theme: Remember to listen to God.

Have any of you ever forgotten to do something your mom or dad asked you to do? [*Allow the children to respond.*] What happens when you forget? [*A few good stories should emerge at this point.*] Remembering to do the things Mom and Dad ask can be pretty difficult. Sometimes it is easy to start playing and forget all about whatever you were asked to do. Sometimes someone asks me to do something, and I try my best to remember—but I just forget. I do not like to forget things either. It seems like every time I forget something, I get into a whole bunch of trouble. I really do not like getting in trouble. Do you like getting into trouble?

To help me to remember, I always carry this in my coat pocket. [*Display the tape recorder.*] Can anyone guess what this is? Exactly. This is a pocket tape recorder. If you look closely, you can see the tiny cassette tape inside. With the help of this tape recorder, I can remember everything!

Suppose (name) tells me, "Rob, my friend Rachel is in the hospital. She must be very sick." Then, all I would have to do is tell my tape recorder, "Rob, go and see Rachel in the hospital." At the end of the day, I play my tape and listen to all of my messages. [*Demonstrate.*] The tape recorder reminds me to visit Rachel. With the help of the tape recorder I can always remember to do whatever I am supposed to do. Now I do not have to worry about getting into trouble anymore.

Even more important than listening to this tape recorder, it is important that we listen to *God*. If we listen carefully to God, we can always remember to do what is right. In fact, the more we listen to God, the less we will have to worry about getting into trouble. Let's ask God to help us remember to always listen to him.

Dear God, help us to remember to listen to you. Amen.

10
The Finest Perfume

Text: "Beloved, let us love one another; for love is of God, and he who loves is born of God and knows God" (1 John 4:7).

Object: Perfume

Theme: Christians fill the air with God's special love.

Can anyone tell me what I have with me this morning? [*Allow the children to respond.*] Maybe a few of you would like to sample this perfume and tell me what you think of its smell. [*There should be plenty of volunteers. A spray bottle of perfume is probably best so you can quickly dispense perfume to those who ask for it.*] Do you like the smell of perfume? [*Allow the children to respond.*] I think this is a nice-smelling perfume. In fact, it's one of my favorites. When I smell this perfume I think of my wife, Janet, because she wears it most of the time. Maybe your mother wears a special perfume that makes you think of her when you smell it. Sometimes just smelling a perfume makes you feel good, because it reminds you of someone you love.

I like being close to this perfume because it fills the air with such a nice smell. Smelling this perfume reminds me of something else I love to be near. I love to be close to Christians. Christians are people who are filled with God's love and that makes them nice to be around. I hope each of you will discover what it means to have God's love in your heart and then you too can fill the air with God's special love like a nice-smelling perfume.

Dear God, thank you for perfumes that are so nice to be near. But thank you even more for Christians who are nice to be around, because they fill the air with your special love. Amen.

11
The Lesson of the Raisin

Text: "Blessed is the man who endures trial, for when he has stood the test he will receive the crown of life which God has promised to those who love him" (James 1:12).

Object: Raisins

Theme: No matter what happens to us, we should also try our very best to make something good happen.

This morning I have something good to eat with me. How many of you like raisins? [*Allow the children to respond.*] Raisins are delicious and they are also good for you.

Can anyone tell me where raisins come from? [*Allow the children to respond. If no one knows, supply the answer.*] That is a pretty hard question. Raisins come from grapes. Do you think this raisin looks like a grape? [*Show a raisin and wait for a response.*] No, I agree. Raisins do not look like grapes. How do you suppose a grape becomes a raisin? [*Children's responses may be varied. Take a few suggestions and then continue.*] Right. Raisins are grapes that have been placed in the sun to dry.

Looking at this raisin helps me to remember a wonderful story about the man who turned a very bad situation into a very good situation. This man was a farmer in California who was known for growing big, beautiful, juicy, and delicious grapes. One time where he was growing his big and juicy grapes something that is very important for plants to grow did not come. Can anyone guess what that might be? [*Allow the children to respond.*] Exactly. It did not rain. He kept hoping it would rain, but it never did.

Pretty soon all the grapes began drying on the vine. The poor farmer was very sad, because he knew there would not be any juicy and delicious grapes to sell. As bad as everything looked for his grapes, the farmer decided to try to make the best of this situation. So he picked all the grapes and laid them out in the sun to dry. What do you suppose happened? [*Allow the children to respond.*] Right! The grapes turned into delicious raisins. So our story ends with a happy farmer who has plenty of raisins to sell—all because he did his very best to make something good happen out of a bad situation.

Whenever I eat raisins I think about that farmer and the important lesson he taught all of us. No matter how bad something may seem—no matter how terrible a situation may be—if we try our very best we can make something good happen.

I have a little box of raisins for each of you. As you eat your raisins after church, think about the important lesson of the farmer. No matter what happens to us, we should also try our very best to make something good come from it.

Dear God, when we are facing a terrible situation help us to always try our very best to make something good happen. Amen.

12
Doing Our Job

Text: " '. . . You shall love your neighbor as yourself' " (Matt. 22:39).

Object: Stapler and several sheets of paper

Theme: Our important job is to do our very best to love each other.

I have something with me this morning that I always keep close at hand in my office. Can anyone tell me what this is? [*Allow the children to respond.*] Right. This is a stapler. I use this stapler almost every day. How many of you have ever used a stapler? What does a stapler do? [*Allow the children to share.*] Correct. A stapler holds paper together. Let me show you how. Inside this stapler [*open the stapler*] there are hundreds of little staples lined up just waiting to do their important job. When we take several sheets of paper like this and press the stapler together, out comes a staple that bends to hold the paper together.

When I think of every single little staple lined up to do its important job, I am reminded of a very important job every single one of us has to do. Did you know all of you have a very important job to do? Yes, [*give the names of three or four children*] and all of you here have a very, very important job to do. Our important job is to do our very best to love each other. Like a staple that holds paper together, when we love others we hold our whole world together.

Next time you use your stapler, think of the important job every staple has, and then remember, like each staple, every single one of us has an important job to do. Our important job is to do our very best to love each other.

Dear God, help us to do our best in our important job of loving each other. Amen.

13

Needed Training

Text: "To equip the saints for the work of ministry, for building up the body of Christ, until we all attain to the unity of the faith and of the knowledge of the Son of God, to mature manhood, to the measure of the stature of the fulness of Christ" (Eph. 4:12, 13).

Object: Running shoes

Theme: Learning to live the Christian life takes training.

Today is my lucky day boys and girls! Do you see what I have with me this morning? [*Allow the children to respond.*] Right, these are shoes. These shoes will make you run very, very fast. Do you know how I know that? I have seen the boy who owns these shoes run. His name is Bill. He is on the track team and he uses these shoes to run very fast in races. When he puts these shoes on he can run really fast. Do you know what I am going to do? I'm going to wear his shoes so I can run fast too. Do you think if I put Bill's shoes on I will be able to run as fast as he does and maybe even win a race too? [*Allow the children to respond. When a child points out that just wearing the shoes does not make you run fast, continue.*] Do you mean to tell me that just wearing these shoes is not going to make me run fast? But when Bill wears these shoes, he can run very fast. Why can't I? [*Allow the children to make suggestions.*] Oh, I see what you are saying. Just wearing the right shoes will not make me run fast. Learning to run fast takes lots and lots of practice. That kind of practice is called *train-*

ing. Learning to run fast enough to win a race takes lots and lots of training. The more I train by practicing my running the better the chance that someday I might be able to win a race.

Did you know, boys and girls, that we have training right here in our church? It's not the kind of training that teaches you how to win a foot race. The kind of training we teach is how to win at living the Christian life. Like learning to run, learning how to live the Christian life takes lots and lots of practice. Just like the runner who becomes better and better because he or she trains, a Christian becomes better and better because he or she trains. The most wonderful result about training as a Christian is that we become the very best we can be for God.

Dear God, help us to remember the importance of training so that we can be the best for you. Amen.

14
Looking on the Inside

Text: "'I the LORD search the mind and try the heart, to give to every man according to his ways, according to the fruit of his doings'" (Jer. 17:10).

Object: X ray and lighted board

Theme: Remember the importance of looking on the inside to understand a person.

How many of you have ever been to the hospital or to see the doctor? [*Children should respond by sharing some of their experiences.*] It is wonderful to have doctors and nurses. When we are sick, they can help figure out what is wrong with us and maybe help us get well.

As smart as doctors and nurses are, sometimes it is hard to tell what is wrong with you just by looking in your mouth or taking your temperature. That's when this is really helpful. Can anyone guess what this might be? [*Surprisingly, many of the children will know this is a picture of inside of someone's body.*] What a smart group of boys and girls! This is a picture of the inside of someone's body. It is called an X ray. Maybe you can tell me what part of the body this X ray pictures. Look closely and see if you can guess. All the white lines are pictures of the bones inside our bodies. [*Allow the children to respond.*] You are right, (name). This is a picture of someone's chest. A picture like this that can look on the inside of you can be very helpful to a doctor in finding what is making you sick.

Let me ask you something, boys and girls. Have you ever had a friend over to play that did not act very nice? Maybe your friend makes an ugly face at you or says something mean like, "I don't want to be your friend anymore." That's when we need to look on the inside of our friends to see what's wrong. Of course, we cannot look on the inside of someone like this X ray and see all the bones. But we can look inside a person and maybe see what's making them act so ugly. Your friend may have a frown on her face because she is especially sad on the inside and needs some extra love. Or maybe if your friend says something ugly it is because someone said something mean to him and he needs to hear a kind word from you. By giving some extra love or saying something nice, you can help your friend feel much better on the inside.

Next time your friend frowns at you or says something ugly, I want you to remember our talk today. Think about this X ray and the importance of looking on the inside to see what's wrong.

Dear God, help us always to look at what's on the inside so we can really understand our friends. Amen.

15

Keeping Balanced

Text: "The LORD has made everything for its purpose"
(Prov. 16:4).

Object: A balance scale and twelve pennies

Theme: A life kept in balance produces happiness.

As you can see, I have a rather unusual object with me this morning. This is something you do not see every day, but perhaps a few of you may have seen at least one. Can anyone tell me what this is? [*Allow the children to respond.*]

This is called a balance. It's wonderful for comparing the weight of different objects. Let me show you how it works. (Name,) would you please put these two pennies on this little dish? What happened to the balance when (name) put the two pennies on one of the dishes? [*Allow the children to respond.*] Now, what do you think will happen if (name) puts these two pennies on the other dish? [*Allow the children to respond.*] Let's try and see if you are right. You *are* right! When (name) placed the pennies in this dish the other dish did come up. Now both dishes are level. When both dishes are level, we call that being balanced.

Do you think this scale would stay balanced if (name) put two more pennies on her side? No? Why? [*Allow the children to explain.*] Exactly, adding two more pennies to (name's) dish would make her side heavier and it would come down. [*Demonstrate.*] That's called "being out of balance." What do you think I could do to get our scales back in balance? [*Allow children to make suggestions.*] Yes. Add two more pennies to (name's) side.

This is such a smart group. Let me share something with you that will make you even smarter. Even more important then making these pennies balance is having a balanced life. Like balancing these scales, we balance our lives by how we spend our time. Let me show you what I mean. Let's pretend this penny stands for watching television. If all we ever did was watch television, would our lives be balanced? [*Add a coin to one dish.*] No. We can see that our scale is out of balance. But, if part of the time we watch television, and part of the time we do our homework, we balance our time. [*To demonstrate, place a coin on the other dish.*] Playing is great fun, but if we play all the time our life will be out of balance. [*Add another coin to one dish.*] Let's add some work [*another coin*] to this side and see what happens. We are balanced again.

The Bible teaches that living a balanced life is very important. By taking the time to work, learn, and play, we are sure to live happier lives. Let's ask God to help us to live a balanced life by remembering to take time to work, learn, and play each day.

Dear God, help us to keep our lives balanced by remembering to take time to work, learn, and play each day. Amen.

16

Covered with Love

Text: "That he may incline our hearts to him, to walk in all his ways, and to keep his commandments, his statutes, and his ordinances, which he commanded our fathers" (1 Kings 8:58).

Object: Paint, brush, and an old board

Theme: Jesus can make us like new with his love.

At one time or another, probably every one of you has seen what I have with me this morning. Can you tell me what this is? [*Allow the children to respond.*] Of course, this is a brush. I also have some paint with me. A brush without paint is not much good is it? What are some of the things you can paint with a brush like this? [*Allow the children to respond.*] Using a paintbrush like this can be a whole lot of work. Why do you think your mom or dad takes the time to paint the rooms in your house or even the outside of your home? [*Allow the children to respond.*] Yes, a new coat of paint makes everything look so much better. Watch how I make this old board look like new in just a few moments. [*Paint board.*] What do you think of our board now? Isn't it nice and clean and pretty? [*Allow the children to respond.*]

Did you know that when you accept Jesus into your heart, it's like getting a brand-new coat of paint? Just as this coat of paint makes this old board look new, Jesus can make us new. Jesus makes us new by covering us with his love. With Jesus in our hearts we want to be better and we are better. When Jesus lives in our hearts, we say kind words like *I love you*, we do kind deeds by helping others, and we care for those who have special needs like those who are sick and lonely.

Next time you see a newly painted house, think about the difference having Jesus in your heart makes. Remember, Jesus can make you new with his love.

Dear God, thank you for Jesus who makes us new with his love. Amen.

17

There Is a Difference

Text: "A new commandment I give to you, that you love one
another; even as I have loved you, that you also love one
another" (John 13:34).

Object: Identical twins

Theme: Our differences make us special.

I can see some of you are already looking around
wondering where my object is. Actually I have two objects
and you can see them right now. My objects are (name)
and (name). [*Have the twins sit—one on each knee. Practice
before the service is advised!*] Tell me, are you (name) or are
you (name)? Oh, then you must be (other twin's name)!
Have you all noticed how much (name) and (name) look
alike? I wonder why (name) looks like (name) and (name)
looks like (name)? [*Allow the children to respond.*] That's
right! (Name) and (name) are twins.

They look so much alike, it is almost impossible to tell
which one is which. Their hair is the same color. Their
eyes are the same color. Even their noses and ears look just
alike. Do you think there are any differences between
them? [*The response will probably be varied, but most will
feel there are no differences.*]

(Name) and (name) are a lot alike, but they still are different from one another. [*A consultation with the twins'
mother and father is advised to discover the differences before delivering the sermon.*] Look very closely at (name's)

throat. There is a tiny little freckle on his throat. Now look at (name's) throat. Do you see a freckle? No. (Name) does not have a freckle on his throat. The freckle is not the only difference between (name) and (name). I talked to their mom and dad and found some other differences. (Name,) do you like raisins? Oh, I see. You love raisins. How about you, (name)? Do you like raisins? You don't. That is a difference. (Name) likes raisins and (name) does not. Do you both like hot dogs? [*Allow the twins to respond.*] Only (name) likes hot dogs and (name) does not.

Even though (name) and (name) look a lot alike, they are still different. Did you know that God made every one of us different? There is nobody else in the whole wide world that is just like you. No matter where you look you will never find another [*name other children in group*]. Because no one else is just like you, that makes each and every one of you very, very special. Let's thank God for making each of us so very special.

Dear God, thank you for making each and every one of us very, very special. Amen.

18
Asking for Help

Text: "'Ask, and it will be given you; seek, and you will find; knock, and it will be opened to you. For every one who asks receives, and he who seeks finds, and to him who knocks it will be opened'" (Matt. 7:7, 8).

Object: A jar of sugarless gum balls

Theme: If we remember to ask God for his help, every choice we make in life will be much, much easier.

What do you see inside this jar? [*Allow time for a response.*] Right, this jar is filled with delicious gum balls. Have you ever seen so many gum balls? What are some of the colors you see? They sure look good, don't they? I wonder if anyone would like to have one or two or maybe three gum balls? [*The response should be enthusiastic!*] Oh, my goodness, everybody wants some gum balls! Well, you all may have a gum ball or two if you can do one simple thing—guess how many gum balls are inside my jar. I have very carefully counted them and written the number down on the bottom of this jar. If you can guess the number, you all may share the gum balls. Can anybody guess? [*Allow the children to begin guessing.*]

You all are making some pretty good guesses, but I can see it would be pretty hard to guess the exact number. Would you like me to help you? Okay, guess a number, and I will tell you if you are too high or too low. [*Allow the children to guess until the correct number is suggested.*]

You know, boys and girls, it sure was hard for you to

guess the number of gum balls in my jar when you were trying to guess without my help. But when I helped you, it did not take you long at all to guess the right number. Having some help sure makes it easier. Of course, that is true not just with gum balls but with everything. Having help makes everything much, much easier.

There are many people who love you and are just waiting to help you whenever you need it. The greatest help we can receive comes from the one who loves you the very most—God. If we remember to ask God for his help, every choice we make in life will be much, much easier.

I hope you enjoy chewing your gum balls. Meet me here after the service and I'll give you one. [*Pass out the gum balls then.*] As you chew and chew, I hope you will remember that everything is easier with God's help.

Dear God, help us to remember that everything is easier with your help. Amen.

19
The Light of the World

Text: "In him was life, and the life was the light of men" (John 1:4).

Object: Lighted globe

Theme: The source of our power to shine comes from God.

I am sure everyone will recognize the object I have with me this morning. [*Allow the children to respond.*] Exactly. This is a globe. What is a globe? [*Allow the children to respond.*] This is a very nice globe. I like looking at all the different colors. What do you suppose all of this blue represents? [*Allow the children to respond.*] My goodness, look at all the water we have on our world. No wonder an ocean looks so big when you stand on the seashore! Along with all the blue, I see green, brown, and yellow. What do you suppose these colors represent? [*Allow the children to respond.*] You are a bright group. All of these colors represent land. This land is called *Africa*. This land is called *Russia*. And this land is *America*. Where do we live—in Africa, Russia, or America? [*Allow the children to respond.*] Right! We live in America. If you look very, very closely at America, you will even see our state—(name).

This globe is special because it lights up when you turn this switch. [*Turn the light switch.*] Oh, goodness! Nothing happened! That's funny, the globe lighted at home. I wonder what the problem is? [*Allow the children to investigate. They will quickly discover the problem.*] Oh, my, you are right! I forgot to plug in the cord. Let's plug it in and see what happens. Look! Our whole world is lighted!

Did you know that Jesus once said that when we accept him as our Lord and Savior, we become the light of the world? What Jesus meant by that was that when he lives in our hearts, we are so much happier that we sort of shine. If we try to shine by ourselves, without the help of Jesus, it is like trying to turn on this globe without plugging in the cord. What happens? [*Allow the children to respond.*] Right. No matter how hard we tried, nothing happened. But when we plug ourselves into Jesus, we can shine and shine as his little lights. By having Jesus in our hearts, we can help light up our world.

Dear God, help us to remember to plug into Jesus so we can shine and shine as his little lights. Amen.

20

The Good and the Bad

Text: "For this slight momentary affliction is preparing for us an eternal weight of glory beyond all comparison" (2 Cor. 4:17).

Object: Blender, egg, milk, vanilla ice cream, chocolate, small cups

Theme: Both good and bad things can be mixed together to make something great.

I am glad you all are here today. When you find out what we are going to make in children's church you will be glad you are here too. As you can see, I have several different things with me. How many of you like eggs? [*Allow the children to respond.*] I am glad to see that so many of you like to eat eggs. Who would like to eat this egg? [*Break the egg into the blender.*] No one wants to eat this egg? I thought most of you liked eggs. Oh, I see. None of you like to eat raw eggs! Maybe we can improve the taste of this raw egg by adding something else. [*Ask one of the children to help you pour some milk into the blender.*] Milk is really good for you, isn't it? Would anybody like to drink this milk with the egg floating in it? [*Allow the children to respond.*] No one? I guess we will never know if milk and eggs are good together. When I was a little boy, I just loved ice cream. To tell you the truth, I still love ice cream! Do you think adding some good vanilla ice cream will help? Now we have an egg, some milk, and a lot of ice cream. All we need now is a little chocolate. [*Ask one of the children to add some chocolate.*] This is looking better all the time. Let's mix it up and see what we have. [*Have one of the children push the appropriate button.*] Look what we have! [*Children will immediately respond.*] This looks like a great-tasting chocolate milk shake. [*Pour some milk shake into a cup.*] Who would like to try our chocolate milk shake? Everyone! [*Allow one child to sample the milk shake.*] How does it taste? [*The response from the child should be enthusiastic.*]

Did you know that life is a lot like a milk shake? Some days things may happen to you that seem about as bad as eating a raw egg. Maybe you have a bad day because your mom makes you clean up your room. Or maybe your dad makes you go to bed extra early without a bedtime story. That's about as much fun as eating a raw egg. But on other days, things may happen to you that are just great. They are days that are like eating ice cream with chocolate on top. We all have happy days such as when our family goes on vacation to the beach, or when we get to do something special like going to our favorite pizza parlor.

What I want you to remember is that even though we may have some bad days, when we are mad or sad, when we mix them together with our good days, when we feel happy, everything usually turns out great—like our milk shake. So when you drink your milk shake later on, re-member, both good and bad things can be mixed together to make something great. [*Send the blender full of milk shake to your children's worship service with enough small paper cups for all.*]

Dear God, help us to remember that we can mix both the bad and good things that happen to us to make something great. Amen.

21
Puppy Love

Text: "Children, obey your parents in the Lord, for this is right" (Eph. 6:1).

Object: Puppy

Theme: Saying "no" can show love.

This morning I have a very special and new friend with me. What sort of friend is this? [*A quick and enthusiastic response should come.*] Of course, this is a puppy. His name is (name). He belongs to a good friend of mine. Feel how soft he is. Look at his tiny feet, his short tail, and his floppy ears. This is about the cutest puppy I have ever seen. How old do you suppose this puppy is? [*Allow the children to respond.*] (Name) was the closest. (Name) is just ten weeks old.

What do you suppose my friend does to take care of him? [*Children will suggest a variety of things such as feeding, bathing, petting, and playing.*] Do you think my friend will let (name) do anything he wants to do? [*The responses will probably be mixed. Some children will not be sure, some will say yes, and some no. Continue by offering the following questions allowing a response after each one.*] Should he be allowed to play in the street? Why? Should (name) be allowed to eat all the chocolate-chip cookies he wants? Why? You are a smart group. You are right. (Name) might get hit by a car and seriously hurt if he plays in the street. Eating all the chocolate-chip cookies he wants would most likely make him very sick. If we really love (name), sometimes we must tell him no; as when he wants to play in the street or wants to eat too many cookies.

Do your parents ever say *no* to you? [*Allow the children to respond.*] Why do your parents say no? [*A variety of opinions will be given.*] The Bible talks about children obeying their parents because they understand what is best. In the same way we love this puppy and want the best for him, your parents love you and want the best for you. So sometimes they say no to you because they do not want you to get hurt or sick.

I bet my friend will do a great job taking care of (name). I know she will love him and say no when it is best. I hope you will listen to your parents when they say no, and understand that when they say no it is because they love you and want the best.

Dear God, help us to listen to our parents when they say no, and understand that when they say no it is because they love us and want the best. Amen.

22

Sourness and Sweetness

Text: "Count it all joy, my brethren, when you meet various trials, for you know that the testing of your faith produces steadfastness" (James 1:2, 3).

Object: Lemon slices and lemonade

Theme: Sour problems can become sweet opportunities.

Can anyone tell me what sort of fruit I have with me this morning? [*Allow the children to respond.*] Of course, this is a lemon. How many of you have ever tasted a lemon? [*Allow the children to respond.*] I think it is fun to watch others eat lemons. [*Share a couple of slices with the children.*] Why is (name) making such a funny face? [*The children will explain that (name's) funny face is a result of the sourness of the lemon.*] You are right. Lemons are really sour. They are so sour, maybe we should take all the lemons in the world and throw them away. Do you think that would be a good idea? [*Allow the children to respond.*]

Throwing away all the lemons in the world is really a terrible idea. We all know that wonderful things can be made from lemons. Just think, without lemons there would be no lemonade. [*Pour a small cup and allow a child to sample.*] Doesn't that taste great? It is amazing that something so sweet can be made from something so sour.

Sometimes things may happen to you that seem pretty sour—like when a good friend moves away or you get into trouble with your mom or dad. But if you look at your sour troubles in a different way, you can make something really sweet happen. A friend moving away may mean a chance to meet a new friend. Trouble with your mom or dad may help you learn how to be really good the next time.

Next time things seem pretty sour, remember this sour, sour lemon and then think of this sweet, sweet lemonade that came from lemons. Maybe that will help you to remember that when sour problems happen to you, you can make something sweet from your troubles.

Dear God, help us to remember that when sour problems happen to us, we can make something sweet from our troubles. Amen.

23

Transformation

Text: "'Judge not, that you be not judged'" (Matt. 7:1).

Object: Transformer toy

Theme: People are not always as we think they are at first.

You all are so lucky. When I was a child, I never would have believed there could be so many different toys one day. I love going to the toy store and looking at all the different kinds. Don't you? [*An enthusiastic response should come!*]

The toy I have with me today is one that has been around for a few years. Can anyone tell me what kind of toy this is? [*Allow the children to respond.*] Right. This is a transformer. All of the toys I played with when I was a little boy always stayed the same. What I mean is that my red fire engine was always a red fire engine; my bulldozer every single day was a bulldozer; and no matter how many times I played with my train, it was always a train.

Does this toy always stay the same? [*Allow the children to respond.*] You are right. This toy does not always stay the same. Right now, this toy is a ＿＿＿＿＿＿. But watch [*transform the toy*]. Now this toy is a ＿＿＿＿＿＿. Isn't that amazing? First this toy was a robot. Now it is a squirt gun. We must be very careful with this kind of toy and look very closely before we decide what it is. Because what it appears to be when we first see it may change [*transform the toy*] when we look again.

Did you know, boys and girls, it is even more important to be careful when we decide who another person is. Sometimes we may look at a person and say: "I don't like Billy because he looks mean"; or, "I think Sally is unfriendly when she doesn't talk to me"; or, "I think Jimmy is a crybaby because he was crying yesterday." That's when we may need to look again. If we look closely we may see: Billy isn't really mean. He might be having a bad day and need some special understanding. Sally isn't really unfriendly. She is just shy and especially needs you to be extra friendly. Jimmy isn't really a crybaby. He is just sad and needs your kindness.

Looking again is very important because we discover that things are not always like we think they are at first. Like this toy that can change before our eyes, our friends can change too, if we only give them a chance to see them another way.

Dear God, help us to remember that people are not always as we think they are at first. Help us to see them in other ways. Amen.

24

Avoiding a Trap

Text: "Be sober, be watchful. Your adversary the devil prowls around like a roaring lion, seeking some one to devour" (1 Peter 5:8).

Object: Ant trap

Theme: Beware of traps that lead to trouble.

I believe most of you will recognize the object I have with me this morning, although a few of you may have never seen one. [*Allow the children to respond.*] Can anyone tell how an ant trap is used? [*Allow the children to explain.*] Exactly, an ant trap is used to catch ants. Let me show you how it works. First, you punch out holes where the directions say so the ants can go inside. If we were to put our ant trap in the right place, pretty soon an ant would probably come walking along. The ant would see this interesting package with his kind of food inside, and then say to himself, "My, this powder smells sooooo good! I bet it tastes even better!" Would it be a good idea if the ant decided to take a bite of this "food"? [*The children will point out the danger.*] You are right. If the ant takes a bite of this food, he will probably get poisoned by the food in the trap. That would be pretty sad for the ant and his friends who follow him. What do you think the ant should do when he sees this food? [*The children will point out that a smart ant would leave it alone.*] I agree. A smart ant would just leave this alone no matter how good it looks.

Sometimes we are a lot like a little ant. We may see something that looks like fun, but if we go ahead and do it, we might just get into a whole bunch of trouble. Suppose you were playing ball in your front yard and you thought to yourself, "I think playing out in the street would be much more fun." Would it be very smart to run in the street and start playing? [*The children will point out the obvious dangers involved.*] Playing in the street would not be very smart. Or let's suppose you were playing inside and thought to yourself, "I bet it would be lots of fun to climb to the top of this tall chest and jump." Would it be very smart to climb to the top of the chest and jump? [*The children will point out the danger of being injured.*] Climbing and jumping from a high place would not be very smart.

Part of growing up is learning what to do and what not to do. Doing some things like playing in the street or jumping from a high place can be as dangerous for you as it is for the ant who decides to eat the food in our trap. To be like a smart ant we need to learn what kind of things will get us into trouble. How can you learn what you should do and what you should not do? [*Children will suggest listening to teachers such as Mom and Dad, Sunday-school leaders, and so forth.*] Listening to people who love you like your parents and your Sunday-school teachers will help make you very smart. Being smart will help you stay away from traps that lead to trouble. (And, yes, you should not touch an ant trap either!)

Dear God, help us to be smart and stay away from traps that lead to trouble. Amen.

25

The Perfect Bath

Text: ". . . wash away your sins, calling on his name" (Acts 22:16).

Object: Soap

Theme: God's forgiveness cleanses us when we do wrong.

How many of you took a bath either last night or this morning? [*Allow the children to respond.*] Everybody took a bath! Why do you take baths? [*Allow the children to explain.*] Oh, I see. You take baths because you get dirty. How do you get dirty? [*Allow the children to respond.*] Taking a bath makes good sense. It would be pretty silly to put on your nice, clean Sunday clothes when you are covered from head to toe with dirt.

I have something with me that is very, very important for bathtime. Can you tell me what this is? [*Allow the children to respond.*] Of course, this is a bar of soap. Why do we use soap during bathtime? [*Allow the children to respond.*] Exactly. Soap washes away all the dirt. Isn't it a great feeling to climb out of the tub nice and clean? It is an especially good feeling when you have been covered from head to toe with dirt.

Did you know that there is something even better than the good feeling you get after a bath? That feeling comes after you know God has forgiven you. Have you ever done something you know is wrong? [*Allow the children to respond.*] How does that make you feel? [*Allow the children to respond.*] Right. When we do something we know is wrong, we feel like we have dirt all over us. That can be an awful feeling. That's when we need forgiveness. Can anyone tell me what forgiveness is? [*Allow the children to explain.*] Forgiveness is what God gives us when we say we are sorry for something we have done wrong. By asking for forgiveness, God can wash away that bad feeling, and we can once again feel clean all over.

Dear God, thank you for your forgiveness that cleanses us when we do wrong. Amen.

26

God's Special Care

Text: "'. . . Fear not; you are of more value than many sparrows'" (Luke 12:7).

Object: Bird

Theme: God loves us in a special way like no other animal in the world.

One of the most wonderful things about the world we live in is the many, many animals, and this includes birds. Every day we see different kinds of animals—some that crawl, some that run, and some that fly. This morning I have an animal that can fly—a bird. The bird is one of my favorite kinds of animals. In fact, I have a feeder outside my kitchen window where I can watch beautiful birds fly in and out for food.

Let's look closely at this bird and see the great care God has taken in making this bird. Why do you suppose this bird has wings? [*Allow the children to explain.*] You notice the bird also has a long tail. Can anyone tell me why this bird has a tail? [*Explain that the bird needs a tail for balance.*] This bird is covered with soft and colorful _____. Right, *feathers*. Feathers are very important. Do you know why? [*Allow the children to respond.*] Exactly, feathers help keep the bird warm. Our bird, too, has very special feet much different from our own. Why do you suppose his feet are made different? [*Allow the children to respond.*] Right. His special feet helps the bird to hold on to branches so he will not fall out of trees. This bird also has a mouth that is very different from your mouth. What is the mouth of a bird called? [*Allow the children to respond.*] Right—a beak. A bird's beak is very hard and that makes it handy for breaking open seeds. All the time we have been talking, this bird has been watching us very closely with his eyes. Eyes are also important to a bird because the eyes enable the bird to see objects far away. Isn't it wonderful to know God has given so much to this bird—a mouth, eyes, feathers, feet, and wings?

When I think of how much God has given this bird, I remember how much God has given to each of us. God has given us even more than this bird. Not only do we have feet, hands, mouth, and eyes, God has also given us minds to think, hearts to love, and friends and family to share our lives. Knowing how much God has done for us tells us how special we are to God. God loves us more than any animal in the world. Next time you see a bird flying high in the sky, think about how special that bird is to God and then remember, that you are even more special to God.

Dear God, thank you for the birds that remind us of how special we are to you. Amen.

27

A Closer Look

Text: "'But even the hairs of your head are all numbered'" (Matt. 10:30).

Object: Magnifying glass

Theme: No matter how closely God looks at us, no matter what he sees, we can also be sure that he loves you and me.

I can take a really close look at everybody with the object I have with me this morning. Can anyone tell me what this is called? [*Allow the children to respond.*] Right. This is a magnifying glass. Does a magnifying glass make everything look big or small? [*Allow the children to respond.*] Exactly. A magnifying glass makes everything look big— much bigger than what you are looking at really is. Because magnifying glasses can make things look so much bigger, they can be a great help when you need to look very closely at something.

Let's take a moment and look closely at (name's) hand. Without the magnifying glass, we see four fingers, a thumb, and the palm of his hand. But when we hold the magnifying glass over his hand, we not only see his fingers, thumb, and palm, but we can now see hundreds of little lines, tiny hairs, and even a scratch that is just about ready to disappear. Isn't it great to have a magnifying glass like this, when you want to see very clearly?

Do you think God needs a magnifying glass to look

really close at us? [*Allow the children to respond.*] You are right. God does not need a magnifying glass to look close at us, but God does look closely at us. The Bible tells us that God looks so closely at us that he knows even the number of hairs on our heads. What that means is God knows everything about us. God can see the good in us. And, God can see the bad in us. But no matter how closely God looks at us, no matter what he sees, we can also be sure that he loves you and me. Let's thank God not only for taking the time to look very closely at us, but also for loving us when he looks so carefully.

Dear God, thank you for taking the time to look very closely at us, and for loving us when you do look at us like that. Amen.

28

An Awful Mess

Text: "If we confess our sins, he is faithful and just, and will forgive our sins and cleanse us from all unrighteousness" (1 John 1:9).

Object: Fountain ink pen and jar of disappearing ink

Theme: God's complete forgiveness of our mistakes.

A long time ago, when your grandmother and grandfather were children your age, pens did not have ink inside them when you bought them at the store. So when you bought a new pen like this one, you also had to buy a jar of ink so you would have ink to put inside of your ink pen. [*Show the pen without ink and the jar of ink to the children.*]

I am sure most of you have never seen ink in a jar. Would you like to see what the ink looks like inside this jar? [*Allow the children to respond.*] We must be very careful with this ink because it can make a terrible mess. This lid is so tight I don't know if I can get it off or not. [*Using plenty of facial expression, turn the lid. As the lid comes off, spill a portion of the contents on a child. You will want to clue this child in on the secret in advance to keep him/her from getting upset.*]

Oh, no! What an awful mess! I can't believe I have made such a terrible mistake. Look at (name's) white blouse. It's probably ruined. Wait a minute. What's happening? The ink is disappearing. Look, all the ink is gone. Oh, I forgot to tell you—this is disappearing ink.

Isn't it wonderful to make such a terrible mistake like this and then see it all disappear? Let me tell you something else that is even more wonderful. When you really do make a terrible mistake and you do something you know you are not supposed to do, God can make that mistake disappear. When you tell God that you are really sorry, God forgives and then God forgets your blunder. Like the ink that disappeared after my mistake, God forgives our errors after we make them, and then they disappear. Let's thank God for forgiving our mistakes and making them disappear.

Dear God, thank you for forgiving our mistakes and making them disappear. Amen.

29

Staying Afloat

Text: "For I am sure that neither death, nor life, nor angels, nor principalities, nor things present, nor things to come, nor powers, nor height, nor depth, nor anything else in all creation will be able to separate us from the love of God in Christ Jesus our Lord" (Rom. 8:38, 39).

Object: Life jacket

Theme: Hold on tight to Jesus.

Something very special will happen this week. I wonder if anyone might tell me what it is. Right! Tomorrow begins the last week of school. In only five short days summer vacation will be here.

Summertime sure is a lot of fun. What are you all planning to do this summer? [*Allow the children to respond.*] I am really not surprised that so many of you like to go swimming. Swimming is one of my very favorite things to do also. I especially like swimming in the lake or ocean when the waves are big. Do you all like to swim in big waves? [*Allow the children to respond.*]

I agree with some of you who are saying that swimming in the ocean is scary. That is why I wear my life jacket. With its help, I can float along on top of the water and do nothing but soak in the warm sunshine. Have you ever used a life jacket? [*Allow the children to respond.*] The best part about having one is no matter how deep the water is, you do not have to worry about sinking. As long as you wear it, the jacket will keep you safe on top of the water.

Because of the life jacket, there is really no reason to be scared of the deep water. It will hold you up.

There are plenty of other happenings in life that can be pretty scary—not just swimming in deep water. Sometimes it is scary to make a new friend. Sometimes it is scary to say no to a friend who wants you to do something bad. Sometimes it is scary to tell your parents the truth when you make a mistake or do something they do not like. That is when it is important to hold tight to Jesus. As long as you hold tight to Jesus, you really do not have to be scared of anything. Jesus will hold you up no matter where you are and help you no matter what you have done.

I hope this summer you will spend a lot of time soaking in sunshine. When you are in the water, being held up by your jacket, think about Jesus holding you up, and soaking in the sunshine of his love.

Dear God, help us to remember that Jesus will hold us up. Amen.

30
Leaning on God

Text: "Who shall separate us from the love of Christ? Shall tribulation, or distress, or persecution, or famine, or nakedness, or peril, or sword?" (Rom. 8:35).

Object: Crutches

Theme: Leaning on God gives time for our hurts on the inside to heal.

I just can't tell you how much trouble I went to to get my object this morning. Surely none of you have had to use these before, but probably all of you have seen some of these before and know what they are called. [*Allow the children to respond.*] Right. They are called *crutches.*

If you watched closely as I came over to join you in children's church, you already know why I am using these crutches. [*Children will explain that crutches enable a person to walk.*] Exactly. These crutches are helping me to walk. But last week I was walking without crutches. Why do you suppose I need crutches this week? [*Allow children to venture some guesses.*] This is a smart group. The reason I am using crutches is because I hurt my leg last week and because of the injury, my leg is not strong enough to hold me up. Silly as I feel using these crutches to walk, they really are very, very helpful because I can lean on my crutches and therefore not use my leg. That's great because I can still walk, using my crutches and at the same time give my leg the time it needs to heal.

Having to lean on these crutches to walk helps remind me of how much I need to lean on God to live my life. Like these crutches that I lean on to walk, we can lean on God for help. Leaning on God assures we can face whatever may happen to us in life. So the next time you see me or someone else leaning on a crutch, think about God and how much we all need to lean on him to live our lives.

Dear God, thank you for being there to lean on when we hurt on the inside. Amen.

31
Loving Care

Text: "'. . . Observe how the lilies of the field grow; they do not toil nor do they spin, yet I say to you that even Solomon in all his glory did not clothe himself like one of these'" (Matt. 6:28, 29).

Object: A bouquet of flowers

Theme: God loves and cares for each and every one of us.

Something wonderful is happening everywhere we look these days. Tree branches are filled with little buds. Soon they will become beautiful leaves. The grass that has been brown all winter is now green and beginning to grow. Even the sun feels warm, and we know that soon there will be many hot days to enjoy. Why is all this happening? [*Allow the children to respond.*] Of course, this is the time when all of nature comes back to life. What do you all like best about spring? [*Allow adequate time for the children to share their appreciation of spring.*]

As you can see, I have a bouquet of flowers with me. They are pretty, aren't they? Would each of you like to have one? [*As you are handing out the flowers continue with the message.*] Jesus once talked about flowers. He asked us to look carefully at the flowers and to realize how beautiful God had made them. Knowing what a good job God has done taking care of these little flowers, Jesus taught us that we can be certain God will do a good job of taking care of us also.

Everyone is looking at his or her beautiful flower, but please take a moment and look at the person next to you. Even more than God cares for your flowers, God cares for each one of you. Everyone of you are an expression of the love and care of God. Let's thank him for loving and caring for each and every flower, but, even more important, let's thank him for loving and caring for each and every one of us.

Dear God, thank you for loving and caring for each and every one of us. Amen.

32

The Sweetest House

Text: "But the fruit of the Spirit is love, joy, peace, patience, kindness, goodness, faithfulness, gentleness, self-control; against such there is no law" (Gal. 5:22, 23).

Object: Gingerbread house

Theme: Jesus gives us the right kind of stuff to build our lives.

I wonder if any of you have ever seen a house like this one? What would you need to build a house like this house? [*Children will point out the many wonderful candies and cookies that make up your little "home."*] Do you suppose we could build a pretty candy house like this with green beans, corn, or potatoes? [*Allow the children to respond.*] You're right; in order to build a house like this we must use only candy, cookies, and icing.

Can you imagine really living in a house made of candy and cookies? Wouldn't that be great fun! Everywhere you looked there would be plenty of wonderful things to eat. If you should get the least bit hungry, all you would have to do is eat part of your house like maybe a window, door, wall, or roof.

As important as it is to use the right stuff to build a candy house, it is even more important to use the right stuff to build our lives. Jesus gave us the best stuff to use to build our lives when he taught us how to live in peace, love, joy, gentleness, and patience. When we build our

74

lives with wonderful material like peace and love and joy and gentleness and patience, we will turn out even sweeter than this house made of candy.

Let's thank Jesus for giving us the stuff that will build our lives with sweetness.

Dear God, thank you for Jesus who gives us the right kind of stuff to build our lives in order to make us sweet. Amen.

33

The Best Part

Text: "'. . . I came that they may have life, and have it abundantly'" (John 10:10).

Object: Cupcakes and icing

Theme: God is the best part of life.

I hope you all did not have a big breakfast this morning because I have something special with me today. Does anyone like cupcakes? Everybody. That's great! Fortunately, I have enough cupcakes for everyone to have one. [*Wait before handing out the cupcakes.*] As you can see, there is not any icing on these cupcakes. I have been so busy going to church and working that I barely had time to make these cupcakes. At first I thought, "Oh well, it really doesn't matter if there is icing on the cupcakes." Then I started thinking about how good icing tastes. Do you all like the taste of icing? [*Allow the children to respond.*] I really like the taste of icing too. I agree with some of you who have said that icing is the best part of the cupcake.

Well, I remembered to bring some icing with me to children's church. [*Begin icing the cupcakes and continue talking, while handing them out.*] Icing these cupcakes helps me remember the difference God makes in each of our lives. Sometimes we may get busy playing or going to school and think, "Oh, well, I am much too busy. I really don't have time for God." Sometimes we even forget what a difference God makes in our lives. That is when it is important to remember that God is really the best part of each life. To live without God is like having a cupcake with no icing. Just as the icing makes the cupcake taste so wonderful, having God in our lives makes our lives wonderful.

I hope you enjoy your cupcakes this morning. As you enjoy the best part—the icing—I hope you will remember the best way to enjoy life is with God.

Dear God, help us remember the best way to enjoy life is with you. Amen.

34
Good News

Text: "In the beginning was the Word, and the Word was with God, and the Word was God" (John 1:1).

Object: Newspaper and children's Bible

Theme: The Bible gives us the Good News about God.

I am sure everyone can tell me what I have with me this morning. [*Allow the children to respond.*] Of course, this is a newspaper. We see newspapers just about everyday, don't we? Let's look at the front page of this newspaper and tell me what you see. [*Allow the children to respond.*] Right. There are pictures and words in big print and little print.

Why do we have newspapers? [*Allow the children to respond.*] Yes. Newspapers help us learn about what is happening. This newspaper is filled with stories. There are stories about what is happening right here in _____ (your city). And there are stories about what is happening in far away places like California, Africa, and South America. If we had time to read these stories this morning, we would find that some are happy stories, some sad stories, some very exciting stories, and a few funny stories. Stories that tell us what is happening in our world are called "news." Taking the time to read the stories in the newspaper means we are sure to learn about our world.

The newspaper is not the only place we can find news.

Did you know the Bible is full of news? There is so much news in our Bible sometimes we call the Bible the "Good News." Inside our Bible you will find stories and pictures like in the newspaper. [*Open the Bible and show the children.*] Like our newspaper we find that some stories in the Bible are happy stories, some sad stories, some very exciting stories, and a few funny stories.

Do you know what all the stories in the Bible are about? [*Allow the children to share.*] Right, the stories in the Bible are about God. Taking the time to read the stories in the Bible means we are sure to learn about God.

Let's thank God for this newspaper that gives us news about the world and let's thank God too for the Bible that gives us the Good News about him.

Dear God, thank you for newspapers that give us news about our world, and thank you for the Bible that gives us the Good News about you. Amen.

35

Tender, Loving Care

Text: "'O Jerusalem, Jerusalem. . . . How often would I have gathered your children together as a hen gathers her brood under her wings, and you would not!'" (Luke 13:34).

Object: Chick

Theme: The love and care of mother hens reminds us of God's love and care.

Gather around as close as you can this morning. I have an object I am sure you all will want to see. [*Open the box and continue.*] Have you ever seen a cuter baby chicken? Its feathers are so soft it makes her very cuddly to hold. I wonder if anyone might guess how old this little chick is? [*Allow the children to venture a few guesses.*] We have some good guessers, especially _____ (child who guessed closest), because this little chick is only _____ days old.

Where do chickens come from? [*Allow the children to respond.*] Right. Chickens come from eggs. Did you know, before this chick arrived in our world she spent three weeks inside of an egg? Of course during the time our chick was inside the egg, the egg had to be given very special care. The mother chicken, instead of going out to play or taking long walks in the spring sunshine, carefully sat on this egg in order to keep this little baby chick nice and warm while she was growing inside the egg. Even today, after church, I will hurry to take our little chick back to the farm where her mother can keep her safe and warm under her wing. I guess that is the nicest thing about chickens: they care so very much about keeping their little ones safe and warm.

Did you know Jesus once talked about chickens? He told us that God's love is much like the love of a mother chicken. Like a mother hen, God cares so very much about keeping us safe and warm. I guess that is the best thing about God—the way he loves us so very, very much and wants to keep us safe and warm.

Let's thank God for the love and care of mother hens that remind us of his love and care.

Dear God, thank you for the love and care of mother hens, which remind us of your love and care. Amen.

36

Coming Out

Text: "'Peace I leave with you; my peace I give to you; not as the world gives do I give to you. Let not your hearts be troubled, neither let them be afraid'" (John 14:27).

Object: Turtle

Theme: It is important to try even when we are afraid.

This morning I have a little friend that has come to visit us in children's church. Can anyone tell me what sort of friend this is? [*A quick response should be in order.*] Of course, this is a turtle. His name is "Boxer," which is a pretty good name because this is a box turtle.

Boxer has something very hard that covers his entire body—on top, on the sides, and even on the bottom. What is this hard stuff called? [*Allow the children to respond.*] Right. This is a shell and it is just about as hard as a rock. [*Allow the children to feel the turtle's shell.*] Why do you suppose Boxer has a shell? [*Children will probably give a variety of answers, such as a place to hide, a home, to keep the rain off, and so forth.*]

Boys and girls, I brought Boxer with me today so he could meet all of you and become your friend too. [*If the turtle remains in his shell, continue with the following thought.*] So come out of your shell now, Boxer, and meet all the children. Boxer, please come out. Why do you suppose Boxer is staying inside his shell? [*Allow the children to respond. However, if the turtle comes out of his shell, use this thought.*] Oh, I am so glad Boxer came out to meet all of you. I thought Boxer would be a little afraid of being here in a new place with new people he does not know. I am glad he is brave enough to come out of his shell and make some new friends.

Tell me something, boys and girls, have you ever been afraid of doing something new like: making a new friend; spending the night away from home; the first day of school with a brand-new teacher; or taking a bite of peas, okra, or maybe even spinach? It is okay to be afraid of doing new things—but it is important to go ahead and try anyway. If we hide inside a shell like Boxer, we may miss the opportunity to experience something very special, like making a new friend, trying a new food, or enjoying a new class.

Let's remember, boys and girls, sometimes you will be afraid to try something new. When you are afraid, think of our friend Boxer, and remember how important it is to try.

Dear God, help us remember how important it is to try even when we are afraid. Amen.

37
Becoming

Text: "But our commonwealth is in heaven, and from it we await a Savior, the Lord Jesus Christ, who will change our lowly body to be like his glorious body, by the power which enables him even to subject all things to himself" (Phil. 3:20, 21).

Object: Caterpillar

Theme: All of us can change into something better.

This morning I have a little friend with me inside this jar. I wonder if you can tell me what sort of friend this is? [*Allow the children to respond.*] Of course, my little friend is a caterpillar. Caterpillars make great friends because they are fun playmates. They never bite. They feel funny when they crawl up and down your arm. And they are fun to look at because they are so fuzzy and colorful.

Tell me, do you think this caterpillar is always going to be a caterpillar? [*Allow the children to respond.*] No? What will it become one day? [*Allow the children to respond.*] You all are so smart. You are exactly right. One day our little fuzzy caterpillar will turn into a beautiful butterfly. Isn't it hard to believe that one day this little fuzzy worm will become a beautiful butterfly? But we all know that one day it will because butterflies are what caterpillars are meant to become.

As hard as it is to believe this fuzzy little caterpillar can change into a beautiful butterfly, sometimes it is even harder to believe our friends can change and become something better. Have you ever heard others saying things like: "That Wes is so mean. I guess he will always be that way," or "Kristen is so unfriendly. I guess she will always be that way."? [*Allow the children to respond.*] Thinking people will never change is very sad because chances are if we think that way, we will never give them a chance to change.

If you start thinking that someone cannot change, think of the caterpillar that changes into a beautiful butterfly. That will help you to remember that it is always possible for anyone to change into something better.

Dear God, thank you for caterpillars that change into butterflies and remind us that all of us can change into something better. Amen.

38

A Great Attraction

Text: "Be glad in the LORD, and rejoice, O righteous, and shout for joy, all you upright in heart!" (Ps. 32:11).

Object: Magnets

Theme: Being the kind of magnet that pulls others toward us.

Ever since I was a little boy, I have enjoyed playing with these. Can anyone tell me what they are? [*Allow the children to respond.*] Right. These are magnets. Magnets are fascinating and sort of strange. I'm not sure how they work, but watch. If I hold this magnet like this, what happens? [*Allow the children to explain.*] Right. This magnet pulls the other magnet right over next to it. You can even pick the magnet up in the air like this and the other magnet continues to hold on tight. But, if I turn my magnet over like this, what happens? [*Allow the children to explain.*] Right. Now this magnet pushes the other magnet away. No matter how hard I try, the other magnet keeps moving away from the magnet in my hand.

Watching these magnets helps me remember something about each of us. If we turn our mouths this way, everyone can see nice smiles on our faces. When we have smiles on our faces, others are pulled toward us just as when I turn the magnet this way. [*Demonstrate.*] In fact, when we smile we can always be sure others will want to be as close as they possibly can. But, if we turn our mouth this way, everyone can see ugly frowns on our faces. Do you think others will want to be close to us if we look like this? [*Make an ugly frown. Allow the children to respond.*] No. We will surely push others away like this magnet with an ugly frown. [*Demonstrate.*]

Each day we just have to decide what kind of magnet we will be. We can be a magnet like this and push others away. [*Demonstrate by making a frown and using one magnet to push the other away.*] Or we can be a magnet like this and pull others to us. [*Demonstrate by making a smile and using one magnet to pull the other toward it.*] Let's ask God to help us be the kind of magnet that pulls others to us.

Dear God, help us be the kind of magnet that pulls others to us. Amen.

39
True Love

Text: ". . . you yourselves have been taught by God to love one another" (1 Thess. 4:9).

Object: Well-worn doll

Theme: No matter how worn they may look on the outside, on the inside people who love will always feel very, very special.

I wonder, do any of you have a favorite stuffed animal or doll? [*Allow the children to respond.*] What makes your favorite stuffed animal or doll so special? [*Allow the children to share.*] The baby I have with me this morning is Amy's favorite doll. Her name is Mandy. Ever since Amy was born, just about everywhere Amy goes Mandy goes too. Mandy is very, very special to Amy. One time she left Mandy at church. We looked and looked and looked at home and then had to come back to the church to find Mandy so Amy could have her favorite doll at bedtime.

As you can see, Mandy is getting pretty old. Just about all of her clothes have disappeared. Two times one of her hands fell off and we had to tie it back on. I can't tell you how many baths she has had in the washing machine. Even though she is old and a little shabby, Amy still loves her best. We have lots of other beautiful stuffed toys at our home, but Mandy will always be Amy's truest love. Do you know why? [*Allow the children to respond. Pick up on the children's ideas and continue with the following thought.*]

Amy loves Mandy so much because they have shared so much together. Mandy is very, very special because she has always been there for Amy: ready to spend lots of time playing with her; ready to be held when Amy is sick; and ready to be cuddled when Amy is sad.

I think some people are a lot like your favorite doll or stuffed animal. Like your doll or stuffed animal, some people are very, very special because they are always there for you—ready to spend lots of time playing and laughing with you—ready to hold you when you are sick— and ready to cuddle you when you are sad. Sometimes people who love the very most look a little worn and shabby like Mandy. That is because sharing lots of love takes lots and lots of giving. Jesus taught the most wonderful thing about loving and loving and loving some more is that no matter how worn we may look on the outside, on the inside we will always feel very, very special.

Let's thank God for people like Mandy who are always there and always ready to love.

Dear God, thank you for people like Mandy who are always there and always ready to love. Amen.

40
Hitting the Mark

Text: "I press on toward the mark for the prize of the upward call of God in Christ Jesus" (Phil. 3:14).

Object: Dart board and darts

Theme: Learning to love and share takes practice.

Some of you may be familiar with the game I have this morning. Can anyone tell me what this game is called? [*Allow the children to respond.*] Right. This is a game of darts. These sharp, pointed objects that look like arrows are called darts. This round board is called the dart board. The way your parents or older brothers and sisters play this game is to stand back from the dart board about ten feet and throw the dart to the board.

Notice the round circles on the board. The outside circle has a _____. [*Point to each number and have the children tell you the number.*] Right, a ten. The next circle has a _____ (twenty-five). Then a _____ (fifty), a _____ (seventy-five), and this small inner circle is worth _____ (one hundred). Which circle—the ten, twenty-five, fifty, seventy-five, or one hundred—do you think would be the hardest to hit with the dart? [*Allow the children to share their answers and explain.*] The smallest circle is the hardest circle to hit. That is why it is worth so many points. Learning to hit this small circle demands lots and lots of practice.

Jesus taught that the best things in life take a lot of

effort and practice. For example, learning to love and share is as hard, or even harder, than learning to hit the small inner circle of this dart board. But if we practice and practice and practice we can learn to love and share. The wonderful thing about practicing to love and share is that you feel so good about yourself. Like the good feeling that comes from hitting the small circle on the dart board and winning the most points, we feel good when we learn to love and share because we are closer and closer to being a real winner.

Dear God, help us to practice and practice to love and share so that we can be winners. Amen.

41

In Living Color

Text: "May the God of hope fill you with all joy and peace in believing, so that by the power of the Holy Spirit you may abound in hope" (Rom. 15:13).

Object: Box of crayons, paper

Theme: Without colors the world would not be a bright and cheerful place.

Do you all know what I have with me this morning? Of course you do! These are crayons. Let's see, boys and girls, what pretty colors they make. (Name,) would you pick a crayon and color on this piece of paper? What color does this crayon make? (Name,) pick another crayon for us and let's see what color it makes on our paper. That crayon sure makes a pretty bright orange doesn't it? Maybe (name) will pick one more color for us. (Name) picked the blue crayon. That's one of my favorite colors.

Everything we see has color, doesn't it? [*Give a few examples like the carpet and their clothes.*] Boys and girls, wouldn't it be terrible if everything was just black and white? Can you imagine how ugly the trees would be if they were all black, and the grass if it was all white? Yuck! That would be awful, wouldn't it? So when you say your prayers and you are thanking God for your home and your parents, don't forget the small things like thanking him for colors.

Dear God, thank you for these children here today. And Lord, thank you for letting us see the colors, because without colors the world would not be a bright and cheerful place. Amen.

42

A Brighter Light

Text: "'Let your light so shine before men, that they may see your good works and give glory to your Father who is in heaven'" (Matt. 5:16).

Object: Lamp with a three-way bulb

Theme: Shining brighter and brighter with happiness, love, and thoughtfulness.

It's kind of dark in here. Why don't we turn on this lamp. What is wrong? [*Allow the children to respond.*] Of course, there is no light bulb in this lamp. Without a light bulb this lamp cannot possibly shine. Thank goodness I happen to have a light bulb in my pocket. Let's screw the bulb in the lamp and see if it makes a difference. [*Turn on the light.*] Good. Now we have plenty of light.

In the Bible, Jesus taught us that we should let our light shine before others. Of course, we cannot shine like this lamp, can we? [*Allow the children to respond.*] What Jesus meant was that we can shine with happiness, thoughtfulness, and love, because Jesus is part of our lives. Trying to shine without Jesus, is about as hard as trying to make this lamp shine without a light bulb. No matter how hard we try, we just cannot shine.

This light bulb is kind of special. Each time I turn the switch it gets brighter. That reminds me that as Christians we can shine brighter and brighter for Jesus. The way we shine brighter and brighter for Jesus is by doing our very best each day to shine with happiness, thoughtfulness, and love just the way Jesus taught.

Dear God, help us each day to shine brighter and brighter with happiness, thoughtfulness, and love—just the way Jesus taught. Amen.

43

My True Friends

Text: "Beloved, let us love one another; for love is of God, and he who loves is born of God and knows God" (1 John 4:7).

Object: Two friends

Theme: God is our best friend.

[*Have two teens or young adults conduct this lesson.*]

Hi. My name is (first person name). My name is (second person name). And we are friends. Do any of you have friends? [*Allow the children to respond.*] What are some of the things you like to do with your friends? [*Allow the children to share experiences.*] Why do you think friends are important? [*Children should give a variety of answers that you can reinforce.*]

Friends are very important. I like having (first person) for my friend because I can telephone her (him) whenever I need to talk.

And I like being friends with (second person) because we can have so much fun together.

That's right. Whenever something good happens to me and I feel especially happy, I just can hardly wait to tell my good friend (first person).

And, when something bad happens to me and I feel especially sad, I can hardly wait to tell my good friend (second person) because she (he) always makes me feel so much better. Don't you think it would be lonely if we didn't have any friends? [*Allow the children to respond.*]

Did you know that even though your friends and our friends are different, we have one friend in common? Does anyone know who that friend is? [*Allow the children to respond.*] That's right. God is our friend. In fact, God can be our *best* friend if we let him. God is always there ready to listen to each of us. Whenever something good happens to you, and you feel especially happy, God loves to hear your good news. When something bad happens to you and you feel especially sad, God hears your bad news and then helps you to feel much better. Don't you think it would be lonely if we didn't have God as a friend? [*Allow the children to respond.*]

Let's thank God for being our best friend.

Dear God, thank you for being our best friend and for always being there whenever we need you. Amen.

Special Days

44

Enough Love?
Valentine's Day

Text: " 'A new commandment I give to you, that you love one another; even as I have loved you, that you also love one another' " (John 13:34).

Object: Candy

Theme: Giving away love is more important even than giving away candy.

Last (day of week) was a very special day. Can anyone tell me what was special about that day? [*Allow the children to respond.*] Of course, everyone knows that last (day) was Valentine's Day. Why do you suppose we have Valentine's Day? [*Allow the children to share.*] You are right. Valentine's Day is a special day set aside to remember those we love most.

What sort of gifts do people usually give on Valentine's Day to show someone just how much he or she is loved? [*Allow the children to respond.*] Right. On Valentine's Day most people give a card or candy to show how much they love someone.

As you can see, I have some candy with me this morning. I brought this candy to share with each of you. It is my way of showing all of you how much I love you. Does everyone like candy? Great! I have plenty to go around. I suppose everyone will want just one piece of candy. No? Some of you would like to have more than one piece. Oh, I see. All of you would like to have more than one piece of candy. Why? [*Allow the children to respond.*] I see. The candy does taste great and really one piece just isn't enough. It is a good thing I have plenty of candy to go around.

You know, candy and love are a lot alike. If you tell someone "I love you," it feels great and always hits the right spot. But like candy, one little piece of love is not enough. Everyone is hungry for lots and lots of love. In fact, the real truth is people are even more hungry for love than candy. Because people are so hungry for love, giving away love is even more important than giving away candy.

As you're eating your delicious Valentine's candy, remember that as hungry as you get for candy, everybody gets even more hungry for love. So be sure to give some love away every day and you will find there is always plenty to give away.

Dear God, help us to remember to give away some love every day. Amen.

45

Surprise!
Easter

Text: "But the angel said to the women, 'Do not be afraid; for I know that you seek Jesus who was crucified. He is not here; for he has risen, as he said. Come, see the place where he lay'" (Matt. 28:5, 6).

Object: Egg, drained through punched needle hole

Theme: On Easter we remember the surprise that Jesus came back to life.

Do you like surprises? [*Allow the children to respond.*] Surprises can be fun because we sometimes get something we did not expect. A wonderful surprise was given on the first Easter when two very sad women went to visit the tomb of Jesus who had died a few days before. Was Jesus in the tomb when the women arrived? [*Allow the children to respond.*] No. Jesus had come back to life. His tomb was empty. Do you think the women were surprised? [*Allow the children to respond.*]

I have an egg with me this morning to help you understand just how surprised Jesus' friends were on the first Easter. We must be very careful with this egg because it has not been cooked. What do you suppose would happen if I dropped this egg? [*Allow the children to respond.*] Wouldn't that be an awful mess! Especially on Easter, when everyone has on such beautiful clothes. But I really need to talk about what's inside this egg. Let me see, let's crack it open on (name's) head and then we can clean up the mess later. [*Hesitate to let the suspense grow and then crack the egg on someone's head.*]

Look! There is nothing inside this egg! It's empty. What a surprise! Everyone of you thought we would have an awful mess on everyone—especially on (name). What a surprise! Just think, as surprised as we were that this egg was empty, the friends who found Jesus' grave empty were even more surprised. That's why Easter is so very special. On this day we remember the surprise that Jesus was not in the tomb but had come back to life.

Dear God, thank you for the surprise you gave us when Jesus came back to life. Amen.

46

Shining Bright
Advent

Text: "You are the light of the world . . ." (Matt. 5:14).

Object: Candle

Theme: Jesus is the light of our lives.

As you can see, this morning I have a candle with me. Candles come in all sorts of shapes, sizes and smells. The color of this candle is _____ [*response*] and it smells like _____ [*response*]. Can you tell me some times we use candles? [*The children should suggest a variety of uses.*] You all have thought of some great ways to use candles.

Have you ever been sitting at home watching television, playing a game, or reading a book at night and all of a sudden all the lights in the house go out? [*A few stories may surface at this point.*] It can be pretty scary when all of the lights go out, and it's so dark you can't see where you are going. What do you suppose would happen if you jumped up and started running around the house as soon as the lights went out? [*Allow adequate time for an explanation.*] Right, you might bump into something and even fall down. Running around in the dark when you can't see where you are going can be pretty dangerous.

Having a candle like this one can be a big help. All your mom or dad has to do is light the candle [*Light the candle at this point.*] Before you know it, the candle will be shining bright, doing the very best it can to give you all the light you need. Because the candle is burning brightly, you can see every step you take. No matter where you go, no matter how dark it is, a person can carry a candle and have the light needed to keep from falling.

During the month of December we are lighting candles in church to help us remember the birthday of _____ [*response*]. Lighting a candle to think of Jesus is a great idea because when we light the candle we can think of Jesus shining bright in each of our lives. With Jesus in our hearts, we don't have to be scared of anything. No matter where you go, no matter how dark it is, Jesus is always with you, shining bright and ready to help you every step you take.

Dear God, thank you for sending Jesus to be the Light of our lives. Amen.

47

Far Away
Advent

Text: "'. . . He who has seen me has seen the Father . . .'" (John 14:9).

Object: Binoculars

Theme: We can see God up close by looking at Jesus.

Sometimes I try to look at things far away but I just can't tell what I am seeing. Have you ever had that happen to you? Maybe you have looked into the sky and wondered, "Is that a bird or a plane up there?" Maybe you have ridden in the car with your family through the country and seen an animal on the other side of a field and thought, "I wonder what kind of animal that is," but you just can't tell because it's so far away. [*The children may suggest a few other examples.*]

When you cannot see things far away, what I have with me today can be a big help. Can anyone tell me what this object is called? Right, these are binoculars. Binoculars are great for seeing people or objects far away. Let me show you how they work. When you look through the binoculars like this, everything you look at appears much closer. I can see (name) in our balcony. With these glasses I can even see her pretty blue eyes. [*Allow a few children to take a peek to illustrate how the binoculars work.*] Isn't it fun to use these binoculars to see things far away?

Sometimes when we think of God we think of someone

very far away. Wouldn't it be wonderful if we could look through these binoculars and see God up close? We can't do that, can we? But we *can* see God up close—not by looking through our binoculars but by looking at Jesus. That's why the Christmas season is so exciting. Because on Christmas Day God sent his Son, baby Jesus, so that all of us could see what God looks like up close.

Dear God, thank you for sending baby Jesus who helps us see you up close. Amen.

48

The Shepherd's Cane
Advent

Text: "And in that region there were shepherds out in the field, keeping watch over their flock by night" (Luke 2:8).

Object: Candy cane

Theme: The candy cane reminds us of the shepherds who came to see and worship baby Jesus.

This is such a special time of year. Have you noticed all the beautiful decorations in our sanctuary? What are some of the objects you see in our sanctuary that remind you of Christmas? [*Allow the children to respond.*] I especially like our Christmas tree. If you look closely, you will see all kinds of ornaments. The ornaments you find on this tree are probably not like the ones you find on your tree at home. Each ornament is very, very special because every ornament tells us something about Jesus. Why do you suppose we have a Christmas tree that tells us about Jesus? [*The children should explain that Christmas is the birthday of Jesus and the tree is to honor his birth.*] Yes. The reason we celebrate Christmas is because we remember the birthday of Jesus.

A long time ago trees were decorated with only cookies and candy. The cookies and candy were carefully shaped and designed to tell everyone who looked at the tree something about the birth of Jesus. Probably the favorite kind of candy to put on the tree was one of these. [*Show the children a candy cane.*] Can you tell me what this is called? [*Allow the children to respond.*] What do you suppose a candy cane tells us about the birth of Jesus? [*Give the children an opportunity to respond. If no one knows the correct answer, continue.*] The candy cane was put on the tree to remind us of the shepherds. Remember the shepherds heard the angels sing about baby Jesus and went to the stable to see and worship him. The shepherds always carried a cane. Not a candy cane, of course, but a real cane. The cane they used was to guide the sheep.

This morning I have two candy canes for each of you. Take one candy cane home to hang on your Christmas tree. Whenever someone comes to visit your home, show them the candy cane on your Christmas tree. Then tell them the special story about how the candy cane is meant to remind us of the shepherds who came to see and worship baby Jesus. What do you suppose you can do with the other candy cane? [*A quick and enthusiastic response should come!*]

Let's thank God for the candy cane that reminds us of the very special shepherds who came to see and worship baby Jesus.

Dear God, thank you for the candy cane that reminds us of the very special shepherds who came to see and worship baby Jesus. Amen.

49

God's Greatest Gift
Advent

Text: "And the angel said to them, 'Be not afraid; for behold, I bring you good news of a great joy which will come to all the people; for to you is born this day in the city of David a Savior, who is Christ the Lord'" (Luke 2:10, 11).

Object: Nativity scene. (Baby Jesus should be kept out of view until the appropriate moment in the message.)

Theme: Without Jesus there would be no Christmas songs, no Christmas story, no Christmas joy.

All of the wonderful music tells us this is a very special time of the year. Can anyone tell me why our sanctuary is so cheerfully decorated and our choir is singing this beautiful music? [*A quick response should be in order!*] Right. Everybody knows that Christmas is just round the corner.

I wonder, what are some of the very special ways your family celebrates Christmas? [*Allow adequate time for the children to share special Christmas traditions in their families. You will discover Christmas to be a very special occasion as children remember trips to grandmother's house, traditional dinner, buying presents, decorating the tree, and so much more.*] It is so exciting to listen and find Christmas to be such a special time. Perhaps someone can tell me why we celebrate Christmas. [*Allow adequate time for a response. When one child mentions the birthday of Jesus, continue with the message.*] Of course, we celebrate the birthday of Jesus on Christmas Day.

As you can see, boys and girls, I brought something with me today that may be a part of Christmas in your home. Does anyone know what this is? [*Many of the children should quickly respond—a nativity scene.*] Maybe you can tell me some of the things you see here. [*Pick up objects one at a time, allowing the children to name them and briefly discuss their significance. Last of all, pick up the empty manger.*] This is a beautiful manger, but there is something missing. [*Children will point out the absence of baby Jesus.*] You are right! How could I have forgotten baby Jesus? [*Bringing baby Jesus into view, continue with the message.*] Baby Jesus is the most important part of Christmas. Without Jesus there would be no Christmas songs, no Christmas story, no Christmas joy. That is because the reason we remember Christmas is God's greatest gift of love when he gave to each of us his Son, baby Jesus.

Dear God, help us to always remember the most important part of Christmas—the birth of your Son, baby Jesus. Amen.

50

Filling the Days
New Year

Text: "So teach us to number our days that we may get a heart of wisdom" (Ps. 90:12).

Object: A calendar for the new year

Theme: On each day of 19_____ remember that every single day is a precious gift from God.

It's great to be back with you in children's church. Just think, we have not been together since last year! [*Allow the children to respond.*] Oh, yes, you're right. We were together last Sunday. Come to think of it last year ended on _____ (day of week). I guess it hasn't been so long after all. Can anyone tell me what year this is? Of course, this is 19____.

This morning I have a brand-new calendar with me. As you can see, this is a very pretty calendar. Look at all of these beautiful pictures of (animals or other scenes). Under the pictures there are several blocks for each day of the month. Why does each block have a number in it? [*Allow the children to explain.*] Right, the numbers tell us the days of the month. What do you suppose will happen on this day? [*Pick out different days in different months.*] No one knows what is going to happen on December 6 or April 5 or May 17? We can't know because none of these days have come yet. That is exciting because that means we can make every day exactly what we want it to be. It is

110

important to remember, as you live each day of the coming year, that every day you see on this calendar is a precious gift from God. Because God has given us every day of our lives we should make the most of every single day.

This year, as you live each day of 19____, remember that every single day is a precious gift from God. What you do each day of the year is up to you. Make the very most of each day, filling each day and every blank on this calendar with wonderful activities that will make both God and you very happy.

Dear God, thank you for the gift of this new year. Help us to make the most of every single day you give us. Amen.